Rainy Days in the Lake District

Rainy Days in the Lake District

Val Corbett

F

FRANCES LINCOLN LIMITED

PUBLISHERS

Frances Lincoln Limited
4 Torriano Mews
Torriano Avenue
London NW5 2RZ
www.franceslincoln.com

Rainy Days in the Lake District

First Frances Lincoln edition 2012

A catalogue record for this book is available from the British Library.

ISBN: 978-0-7112-3247-1

Printed in China

1 2 3 4 5 6 7 8 9

Commissioned and edited by Jane Crawley

PREVIOUS PAGE Elterwater.
RIGHT Essential footwear.

RIGHT Bowness Bay.
'Aren't they open yet?'

6

Preface

When people asked me – as they invariably did – what I was working on, my answer that I was taking photographs for a book on rain in the Lake District was usually met with incredulity. 'Rain?...What?...Are you serious?'

Which was curious, because ask most people what they know about the Lake District and their answer would include 'It rains a lot'. So if rain and the Lake District go hand in hand, it seems strange that the Lakes haven't been photographed more often in the rain. Indeed, looking back at the many artists who have worked here, very few ever chose to paint rain. Maybe it's because rain can be frustratingly hard to depict. As a photographer I now know that there is 'right' rain and 'wrong' rain. However hard it's chucking it down, rain all too often shows up as nothing but a murky haze and the result is just a muddy photo. Back-lit rain, when immediately followed by sunshine, is great for showing up the rain but that doesn't happen too often. Apart from the obvious things that tell us it's raining hard – opened umbrellas, the splashes of heavy raindrops, people taking shelter – it may not look as if it's raining at all, even if the photographer is getting soaked!

Working on this book has been wonderful, a complete change of direction for me. Looking back over more than twenty-five years of being a photographer, I could count the photos I had taken in the rain on the fingers of one hand. And it would only need the fingers of my other hand to count those that included rain. I was fond, probably over fond, of periods of fine settled weather, with early morning mist rising above calm lakes and beautiful mirror reflections. Lovely though the photos were, I'd missed out on the magical fast-changing light of stormy weather that is so much more typical of the Lake District. Since starting this book clouds have become my welcome friends, the blacker and more rain-bearing the better. Also, surprising though it sounds, I've actually enjoyed being out in shocking weather – the feeling of being up against the elements and battling through driving rain, of being just a bit on the nutty side! I have also learnt to treasure those times just after the storms when the clouds are lifting which result in some of the most atmospheric light I have ever photographed.

Being one of a tiny minority of people in the Lake District actually willing it to rain – and the harder the better – was a novel experience. When passers-by commented that it was no day for photography, I wasn't able to conceal a smirk. Of course it's often been uncomfortable, and frequently frustrating, waiting for just that right shot. For instance, lake foreshores feel dismally bleak places to be in driving rain, and just hanging around waiting for something photogenic to happen can be pretty dispiriting. But if I popped off for a coffee it was inevitable that I'd return to find I'd just missed a magical moment, though retreating for a coffee did allow me to dry off and warm up.

I found that whipping off my socks for a quick dry under the table was quite a relief and I could help myself to a pile of paper napkins to stuff into my saturated shoes. As I progressed with the book, I made it a rule to put on wellies and over-trousers from the very start of each trip. The camera, my poor long-suffering Nikon D300, stood up remarkably well. Tucked under my cagoule, it got briefly whipped out for the photo. It still ended up getting worryingly wet, but never failed to perform.

RIGHT The tiny Church of St Olaf's Wasdale, well protected by its encircling yews, can be a place of shelter. This little window is a war memorial to those who tackled the climbs on the massive peaks dominating the valley.

I WILL LIFT UP MINE EYES UNTO THE HILLS FROM WHENCE COMETH MY STRENGTH.

In the main I have tried to portray the lighter side of 'bad weather'. But of course, however much it is affectionately and jokily associated with the Lake District, the rainfall can have a much more serious side, and the sensitivities of those people who suffered in the dreadful floods of November 2009, particularly in West Cumbria, must be recognised. A contribution from my book advance was made to the flood fund set up by the Cumbria Community Foundation.

LEFT A drawing by James Spedding – even Tennyson had to wait for the rain to stop. (*By kind permission of the Master and Fellows of Trinity College, Cambridge*)

11

I still find the statistics (over a foot of rain fell in a twenty-four hour period) almost unbelievable, even in this the wettest region of England.

One final thought, I've been struck by how phlegmatically visitors accept rainy days. They may complain, but it's usually done with a cheerful twist. I think they recognise – even more than we locals – that the area can be particularly beautiful on wet days and they are quick to point out that the very name, The Lake District, is something of a clue to the weather. When taking photos I have been much helped by many willing and good-humoured models, some friends and some complete strangers, who have stoically agreed to stand around in the wet while I fiddled about with my camera. Their cheerfulness demonstrates those endearing characteristics of the British – they're happy not to take themselves too seriously and they're at their best when things get grim!

VERY Wet Sleddale 1½ ❯

13

LEFT Ullswater.
'Rain,rain, and sun! A rainbow in the sky!' (Tennyson).
OVERLEAF Leaves on the track don't stop the drains.

FAR LEFT These might dry if they don't blow away in the meantime.
ABOVE AND LEFT Drip, drip...drips from a rusty old farm gate (above) and a droplet off a window frame (below). 19

LEFT AND ABOVE Buttermere Show.
Herdwicks after the judging line up (left) and time for a crack (above).

THIS PAGE AND RIGHT World Championship Sheepdog Trials, Lowther.
Mud, mud glorious mud! Squelchy Glasto comes to Cumbria.

LEFT Grasmere. A gentle end to an awful day.
ABOVE Rain sweeping up Ennerdale.

THIS PAGE AND RIGHT Making tracks. Grizedale Forest (above left);
Buttermere Show (above centre and right); Knipe Scar, Lowther Valley (far right).
OVERLEAF A poetical moment as cloud lifts and breaks for a sunset over Grasmere.

LEFT Typical fast-changing Lake District weather – rain-washed Martindale.
ABOVE Crummock Water. My artist friend, Dorothy Ramsay, trying to capture
the weather. The rain won – too wet for watercolours!

ABOVE North-east from Newlands Pass. Hail in the driving rain, a forerunner of winter.
RIGHT The St John's Beck inundating the vale bottom.

LEFT Castlerigg Stone Circle.
ABOVE Flooded fields near Keswick. Silage bales swept downstream by the River Derwent.

ABOVE Grasmere Gingerbread? Me too!

ABOVE Ambleside – marching on, ignoring all temptations.
OVERLEAF Seascale.

LEFT Val and Tony –
Ullswater rising fast –
hoping the auto timer
works soon!
RIGHT Yewbarrow and
Dore Head. 'Is *that*
coming our way?'

ABOVE AND RIGHT Sheep have their own strategies (with some help for the youngest).

RIGHT Blelham Tarn, near
Hawkshead. The rainbow
encapsulates the colours
in the landscape.
FAR RIGHT Elterwater towards
the Langdale Pikes.

LEFT Tarn Hows, picturesque even in the drizzle.
RIGHT Esthwaite Water. Wet weather brings out the fishermen.

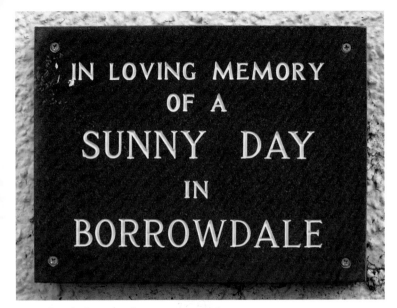

IN LOVING MEMORY OF A SUNNY DAY IN BORROWDALE

ABOVE Seen in Stonethwaite.
RIGHT Scene near Stonethwaite.

LEFT AND ABOVE Fitz Park, Keswick. The benches on the left were taken well back from the bank of the River Greta, ahead of the flood of November 2009. The fixed bench above, close to the river, was festooned with debris after catching the full force of the flood.

LEFT Booth's supermarket, Keswick. Tesco in deep water.
ABOVE Children will play anywhere and anyway.

ABOVE November 2009. One of three ways to Manesty – none open.
RIGHT Ashness Landing Stage, the Keswick Launch operating despite.

FAR LEFT In the event, once the
decorations were up, it turned into
a classic snowy Christmas season.
LEFT Keswick – carrying on
regardless.

November 2009. LEFT Flooded fields near Portinscale.
A William Blake moment – light shining forth on clouded hills.
ABOVE AND RIGHT Borrowdale, the entire valley became a lake.

ABOVE Wild day, looking towards Hartsop.

ABOVE November 2009. The day Derwentwater and Bassenthwaite almost became one.

RIGHT A particularly bleak day at Brotherswater.

ABOVE AND LEFT Ullswater. Sometimes the worst conditions lead to the best photos.

RIGHT My course participants
on an Ullswater Steamer.
FAR RIGHT My husband, Tony,
under orders (as ever!)
to model at the steamer pier,
Pooley Bridge.

LEFT The B5289 in
Borrowdale.
RIGHT The A592
alongside Ullswater.

LEFT Aira Force. There's always
a rainbow on sunny days.
RIGHT Swindale.

ABOVE Derwentwater. Record-breaking rainfall left only the tops of the posts of the landing stage visible. RIGHT Grasmere. 'My heart leaps up when I behold A rainbow in the sky.' (Wordsworth).

FAR LEFT The River Greta at Keswick. Heavy rain means a bonus day for canoeists.
LEFT Potholes, bane of the motorist but fun for some.

RIGHT Magical, ethereal light in Langdale.

FAR LEFT More than
just an April shower
at Dora's Field, Rydal.
LEFT Packhorse bridge
in Great Langdale.

ABOVE Larking around in floodwater at Fitz Park, Keswick.

CENTRE Friar's Crag, Derwentwater

RIGHT Picnic, Tarn Hows.

ABOVE AND RIGHT Bowness-on-Windermere.
Holiday makers making the best of it.

ABOVE AND RIGHT Lovely weather for ducks...

LEFT Wasdale, the last photo of the day.

ABOVE Wasdale. Which way out of here?

FAR LEFT Seen better days? The prom at Maryport.
LEFT Hawkshead.

89

RIGHT Branthwaite Brow, Kendal. A couple under an umbrella

ABOVE Bowness. An odd couple under an umbrella.

LEFT Ullswater. ABOVE Derwentwater. Rain showers backlit by brilliant shafts of sunlight.

LEFT Looking south from Blencathra. ABOVE Windermere.
Turner, Ruskin – no wonder they came to the Lake District
with its ever-changing skies.

LEFT Newlands Valley. ABOVE Looking into Borrowdale.
Typical drifting clouds and rich, saturated colours that follow rain.

LEFT The A66. Leaving the hills behind.
RIGHT Rain. No surprise at Surprise View.

LEFT Rain in Riggindale, at the end of Haweswater, destined to come out of taps in Manchester. RIGHT Two lads, bunking off school, made a bad choice by coming to St Bees on such a desolate day.

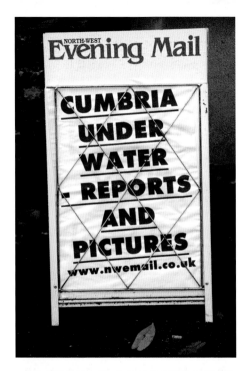

RIGHT November 2009.
FAR RIGHT Jenkin Field, Glenridding.

LEFT AND ABOVE November 2009. Not yet at its worst the storm was already causing havoc at the north end of Ullswater. The steamer pier was badly damaged that night.

RIGHT Bowness-on-Windermere.
Paddling along is the only option.

CRUISE TICKETS

107

ABOVE AND RIGHT Keswick landing stages. Emptying out flooded rowing boats.

ABOVE Keswick Landing Stages – stranded.

ABOVE High and dry – and a long way from home.

RIGHT The upside-down world of a puddle.

RIGHT A revelation at Surprise View.

RIGHT Derwentwater and Skiddaw.
OVERLEAF Rainbow illuminating Derwent Isle,
Keswick behind.

ABOVE Bowness-on-Windermere.

ABOVE Umbrellas – plain black or multi-hued?

ABOVE Snappers snapped.

ABOVE Looking on the bright side.

ABOVE AND LEFT A memorable sight even in poor weather: 'Ten thousand saw I at a glance, tossing their heads in sprightly dance.' (Wordsworth, 'Daffodils')

ABOVE Slate, stone, wood and water – the Lake District.

ABOVE The rain it raineth every day – or so it sometimes seems. Watendlath.

RIGHT Normally seen with blue sky on calendars, postcards, biscuit tins – another view of Ashness Bridge

LEFT Fell-walker pondering the inevitable.
ABOVE Rosthwaite in Borrowdale.

ABOVE Belted Galloway – not happy.

127

ABOVE AND RIGHT Rosthwaite in Borrowdale. Herdwick sheep in the rain – they wait a bit then give themselves a really good shake.

ABOVE Esthwaite Water. Just swanning around.

ABOVE A dogged wait for a bite on Ullswater.

ABOVE I don't suppose they had much of a clue either as to where they were headed.
RIGHT Buttermere Show. Trail hounds ready for the off.

ABOVE AND LEFT Unpromising weather but these campers at Glenridding were clearly not disheartened.

LEFT There's no such thing as bad weather, just bad clothes.

137

LEFT AND FAR LEFT
Cumulonimbus cloud looking
particularly dramatic.

ABOVE The gauge at Seathwaite records the rainfall of the wettest place in England.
RIGHT An outdoor pursuit group not enjoying themselves on Derwentwater. It all ended well.

ABOVE AND LEFT The Great North Swim, Windermere. Warming up in gear as suitable for out as in – and then they're off.

ABOVE Keswick Christmas lights, reflections in the wet paving give added warmth.

ABOVE An acer after rain.

ABOVE Sheltering in bivvies. RIGHT time for a quick brew.
Memorial Sunday on the summit of Great Gable – waiting for 11 o'clock.

LEFT Little Langdale: Bill and Sue Thornton having lunch. I sent them this photo and got bad news by return. While they were walking the following day, their camper van went up in flames where it was parked. They saw the blaze as they crested the last hill on the return. 'We have lost the bus and all its contents – a bit of a shock to use a true English understatement', wrote Bill.

ABOVE Tom Birkett, farming near Threlkeld, took me around his farm on his quad bike and in the course of one hour taught me more than I'd managed to learn in a lifetime about Lake District farming.

ABOVE AND RIGHT In driving rain most sheep head for the shelter of the stone walls ...

but these lambs have gone one better in choosing the lee of the largest stone at Castlerigg Stone Circle.

RIGHT Loughrigg Tarn – too wet even for watersports.

ABOVE Huge raindrops making the surface of Loughrigg Tarn appear to boil.

ABOVE Water on the lily pads after the storm.

LEFT Windermere.

Biography

Val Corbett is a freelance photographer, based in the Lowther Valley on the eastern fringes of the Lake District where she lives with her husband Tony. Over the past twenty-five years she has built up an extensive photographic library of the Lake District and Cumbria (www.valcorbettphotography.com). She is well known for her garden photography, which is frequently published in magazines such as *Country Life. Gardens of the Lake District* (Frances Lincoln), written by Tim Longville and photographed by Val, won the 'Lakeland Book of the Year' award. During the summer she can be found photographing gardens around the British Isles; otherwise she concentrates on her landscape photography, special commissions and working for authors. Three books of her Lake District landscapes have been published by Myriad Press and two, *A Year in the Life of the Eden Valley* and *Winter in the Lake District*, by Frances Lincoln.

LEFT Friar's Crag, Derwentwater. 'I told you we should have gone to Spain.'